225 Fantastic Facts Math Word Problems

by Eric Charlesworth

S C H O L A S T I C
PROFESSIONAL BOOKS

New York • Toronto • London • Auckland • Sydney
Mexico City • New Delhi • Hong Kong • Buenos Aires

Dedicated to my inspirational family
and to Stephanie, who is a good-natured egg.

Acknowledgment
Much thanks to my patient editor Mela Ottaiano.

Cover design by Josué Castilleja
Cover illustrations by Dave Clegg
Interior design by Drew Hires
Interior illustrations by Drew Hires

ISBN 0-439-25618-6

Contents

Introduction

What's in This Book

This book contains 225 word problems that are based on remarkable facts taken from the real world, including world records, historical anomalies, incredible animal facts, and more. Each time a student solves a problem, a new fantastic fact is revealed.

The exercises include addition, subtraction, multiplication, division, fractions, decimals, percentages, and those that require the utilization of multiple skills. All of the problems require the use of conceptual knowledge combined with procedural efficiency. They have been designed to engage students, providing them with extra incentive to find the correct answers.

How to Use This Book

These problems can be used in a number of different ways: as a follow-up to a lesson, as an independent homework assignment, or as a group activity during class. One effective strategy is to assign one question per day, allowing students to stretch their minds at the beginning or end of math period. Working together, the class will enjoy discussing the problems as well as arriving at the interesting answers.

Keeping in mind that over time some fantastic facts change and new world records are set, another helpful exercise is to invite the class to rewrite and recalculate problems using updated information or make up related follow-up problems based on other interesting facts they've heard or read.

Why This Book Works

The answers to the problems in this book actually mean something to students—they're not just random numbers—so students will learn more effectively. When the class takes a natural interest in its math-related work it ceases to be work and becomes something to look forward to. Students become engaged and thereby motivated to attack new challenges and use the same concepts and strategies in all of their math work. The monotony sometimes associated with mathematics will become a distant memory!

How to Meet the Math Standards

The word problems in this book provide dozens of opportunities to meet many of the objectives and expectations throughout Principles and Standards for School Mathematics (NCTM, 2000)—in particular those listed under the Number and Operations standard. These include understanding ways to represent numbers, determining meanings of operations and how they relate to one another, and computing with fluency. This book also helps meet the objectives listed under the Measurement standard, such as understanding the different units of and how to calculate measurement. This book lends itself easily to meeting both the Problem Solving and the Connections standards. Students will practice selecting and using different strategies to solve a variety of problems. Along the way, they'll likely realize that mathematics can be used outside of math class—to help students discover not only everyday information but also amazing facts!

#2

How much did the largest pumpkin weigh?

Clue: Bart weighs 230 pounds. Stephanie weighs 190 pounds. Jenna weighs 130 pounds. Angela weighs 148 pounds. They carved a pumpkin that weighs 12 pounds. Those four people plus the pumpkin they carved weigh the same as the largest pumpkin.

#4

How many points did basketball's all-time leading scorer, Kareem Abdul-Jabbar, score?

Clue: Michael Jordan scored 26,710 points. Abdul-Jabbar scored 11,677 more points than Jordan scored.

#1

How high can insects fly?

Clue: The Empire State Building is 1,450 feet high. Insects have flown up to 2,550 feet higher than the Empire State Building.

#3

How much does the world's largest rubber-band ball weigh?

Clue: The second largest rubber-band ball weighs 850 pounds. The largest rubber-band ball weighs 1,410 pounds more than that.

#6

How many people can the largest plane carry?

Clue: If the plane was full, had a crew of 20 people, and 140 passengers with window seats, then there were 406 passengers who did not get window seats.

#8

Oklahoma is the state in which the most Native Americans live. How many Native Americans live in Oklahoma?

Clue: There are 65,000 Native Americans living in Texas, 80,000 in North Carolina, and 85,000 in Alaska. Oklahoma has 20,000 more Native Americans than those three states combined.

#5

The longest river in the world is Africa's Nile River. How long is the Nile?

Clue: The longest river in the United States is the Mississippi River, which is 2,348 miles long. The Nile is 1,797 miles longer than the Mississippi.

#7

How long is the tunnel a mole can dig in one night?

Clue: A mole digs 60 feet and takes a break. Then it digs 130 feet and takes another break. Then it digs 28 feet and takes a break. Finally, it digs 82 feet and is done for the night.

#10

How many stitches does a soccer ball have?

Clue: A baseball has 108 stitches. A soccer ball has 534 more stitches than a baseball has.

#12

How many skyscrapers are there in New York City?

Clue: There are 47 skyscrapers in Chicago, 27 in Houston, 21 in Los Angeles, and 20 in Hong Kong. But there are 36 more skyscrapers in New York City than in those cities combined.

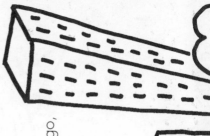

#9

How many square miles are there in Texas's Brewster County?

Clue: Delaware has an area of 2,489 square miles. Brewster County has 3,719 square miles more than Delaware.

#11

The 1996 Super Bowl between Dallas and Pittsburgh had the highest ratings in television history. How many people watched the game?

Clue: If 82 million people watching the game were rooting for Dallas, then 56 million were rooting for Pittsburgh.

#13

How many muscles do you use to frown?

Clue: You use 17 muscles to smile. It takes 26 more muscles to frown than to smile.

#14

How many people played in the largest game of musical chairs?

Clue: After 6,865 people were out of the game, 1,373 people were still playing.

#15

In what year was the cell phone invented?

Clue: The telephone was invented in 1876. The cell phone was invented 103 years later.

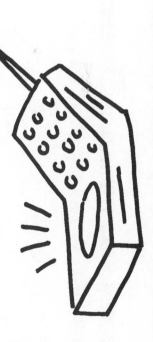

#16

How much time per day does the average American spend watching television?

Clue: Karen spends an average of 1 hour, 19 minutes watching television every day. Karen spends 2 hours, 29 minutes less than the average American spends watching television.

How long was the longest lizard ever discovered?

Clue: Jeff has a beagle that is 2 feet, 6 inches long. The longest lizard was 13 feet, 1 inch longer than Jeff's beagle.

How much money did the movie THE LION KING make?

Clue: Aladdin made $479 million. Toy Story made $354 million. Together they made just $61 million more than The Lion King.

How long was the largest salami?

Clue: Tara's house is 50 feet long, her bike is 4 feet long, and Tara is 4 feet, 9 inches tall. Combined, Tara, her house, and her bike are still 10 feet shorter than the largest salami.

How many videos does the average couple rent in a year?

Clue: Last year, Vicki rented 131 videos and Chris rented 80 videos. Together they rented 173 more videos than the average couple rents in a year.

#22

New York's Coney Island was the home of the first roller coaster built in the United States. In what year was it built?

Clue: Eddie was born in 1972. When he celebrated his twelfth birthday, the roller coaster was 100 years old.

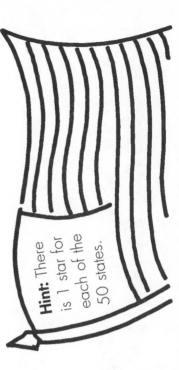

#24

How many stars were on the American flag in 1850?

Clue: Between 1850 and 1900, 16 stars were added. There have been 5 stars added since 1900.

Hint: There is 1 star for each of the 50 states.

#21

In what year was the Internet invented?

Clue: Christina was born in 1987. When she turns 32, the Internet will be 50 years old.

#23

Benjamin Franklin was the oldest man to sign the Declaration of Independence. How old was he when he signed it?

Clue: Franklin signed the Declaration of Independence in 1776. When he died in 1790, he was 84 years old.

#26

The tallest building in the United States is the Sears Tower in Chicago. How tall is the Sears Tower?

Clue: A plane was flying 4,000 feet in the sky, and a skydiver jumped out. After he had fallen 2,000 feet, he was just 550 feet higher than the top of the Sears Tower.

#28

In Japan, Tokyo is the city with the most people. How many people live in Tokyo?

Clue: About 125 million people live in Japan. Of those people, 98 million do not live in Tokyo.

#25

How many presidents were born in Virginia?

Clue: There have been 43 presidents. Seven presidents were born in Ohio, and 28 were not born in Ohio or Virginia.

#27

How many Americans died in the Civil War?

Clue: About 620,000 people live in Alaska. That number is just 120,000 more than the number of people who died in the Civil War.

#30

What is the most weight ever lost by one person?

Clue: This person went from a weight of 1,400 pounds to a weight of 476 pounds.

#32

In what year were eyeglasses invented?

Clue: Contact lenses were invented in 1887, which was 597 years after eyeglasses were invented.

#29

How tall is the tallest tree in the United States?

Clue: A plane is flying at 500 feet. The plane is only 133 feet above the highest branch on this tree.

#31

In what year were blue jeans invented?

Clue: The zipper was invented in 1891, 41 years after jeans were invented.

#34

At what age did the world's oldest person die?

Clue: The oldest person was born in 1875 and died in 1997.

#36

What is the most anyone ever paid for a yo-yo?

Clue: If the buyer paid with $17,000, he received $971 in change.

#33

For how many years was the longest diary kept?

Clue: Ernest Loftus began keeping his diary as a 12-year-old. He wrote in it every day until he was 103.

#35

Theodore Roosevelt was the youngest president. How old was he when he became president?

Clue: The oldest president was Ronald Reagan, who was 77 years old when he left office. When Reagan left office, he was 27 years older than Roosevelt was when he left office. Roosevelt was president for 8 years.

#38

What year was the modern version of the pencil invented?

Clue: The pencil was invented 177 years before the first video game, which was invented in 1972.

#40

How much does your heart weigh?

Clue: Your brain weighs about 48 ounces, which is 39 more ounces than your heart weighs.

#37

How many home runs did baseball legend Willie Mays hit?

Clue: Hank Aaron, who has the most homers, hit 755. Willie Mays hit 95 fewer than Aaron.

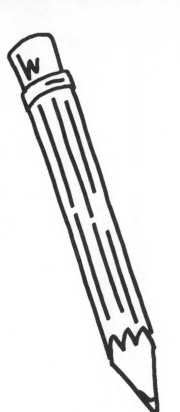

#39

How fast can most pigeons fly?

Clue: Rob was driving his car 63 miles per hour, which is 18 miles per hour faster than most pigeons can fly.

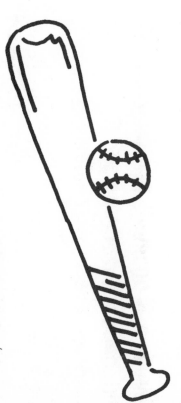

#42

How many feet long were the tentacles on the biggest jellyfish?

Clue: A basketball rim is 10 feet high. The longest jellyfish's tentacles were 12 times that height.

#44

How many times was the world's most-petted dog petted?

Clue: Over a period of 8 years, Josh the Wonder Dog was petted by an average of 59,850 people per year.

#41

How long is a queen termite expected to live?

Clue: A gorilla is expected to live 10 years. A queen termite is expected to live 5 times longer than a gorilla is.

#43

How many decibels is the sound of the loudest whale pulse?

Clue: The sound of a loud crowd cheer in a stadium is about 94 decibels. Whale pulses can be 2 times as loud.

#46

How thick is the ice in Antarctica?

Clue: If you chiseled through the ice in Antarctica at a rate of 4 feet per hour, it would take you 1,625 hours to reach the bottom of the ice.

#48

How many guests could the largest igloo sleep?

Clue: If the largest igloo had 25 rooms, it could fit 4 people in each room.

#45

The most expensive painting ever sold is THE PORTRAIT OF DR. GACHET. How much did it sell for?

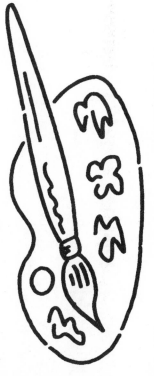

Clue: If someone bought the painting with only $500 bills, the buyer would need 150,000 of them.

#47

How many squares of toilet paper does the average roll contain?

Clue: If it takes 1 week to use 111 squares, the roll of toilet paper will last 3 weeks.

#50

How many radio stations are there in the world?

Clue: There are 7 continents in the world. There is an average of 5,000 radio stations for every continent.

#52

What is the furthest recorded flight of a bird?

Clue: This bird averaged 125 miles per day and flew for 130 days.

#49

How many active volcanoes are there in the world?

Clue: A scientist is planning to see all the active volcanoes in the world. He needs to visit 75 volcanoes per year for the next 20 years.

#51

How much did the largest dinosaur skull weigh?

Clue: Barry weighs 110 pounds. The largest dinosaur skull weighed 40 times what Barry weighs.

#54

The blue whale can weigh more than any other animal. How much can the blue whale weigh?

Clue: The total weight of a group of 4,000 65-pound children equals the weight of a large blue whale.

#56

How many feet high was the tallest cake?

Clue: The cake was divided into 15 layers. Each layer was 7 feet high.

#53

How many calories does the average person take in at Thanksgiving dinner?

Clue: The day after eating Thanksgiving dinner, Cal began a workout that burns 245 calories each day. It took him 8 days to burn off the calories he consumed on Thanksgiving.

#55

How many pounds can an African elephant weigh?

Clue: A ton equals 2,000 pounds. An African elephant can weigh up to 5.5 tons.

How many people work for Wal-Mart nationwide?

Clue: There is an average of 13,500 Wal-Mart workers in every state.

How many pounds of food will you eat in your lifetime?

Clue: An elephant weighs about 10,000 pounds. In your lifetime, you will eat the equivalent weight of 6 elephants.

Quillayute, Washington, gets the most rainfall per year in the continental United States. How many inches does Quillayute get per year?

Clue: Yuma, Arizona, gets the least rainfall, with just 3 inches per year. Quillayute gets 35 times more rain than Yuma.

The country with the fewest people is Vatican City in Europe. How many people live in Vatican City?

Clue: If you divided the people of Vatican City into groups of 20, you would have 42 groups.

The most miles ever driven by one car was by a 1963 Volkswagen Beetle. How many miles did the car travel?

Clue: The distance from coast to coast in the United States is about 3,200 miles. The miles that the 1963 Beetle drove are equal to 500 coast-to-coast trips.

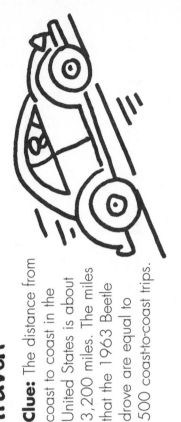

#64

How many stairs are there in the Empire State Building?

Clue: Terry climbed to the top of the Empire State Building at a rate of 93 stairs per minute. It took her 20 minutes to reach the top.

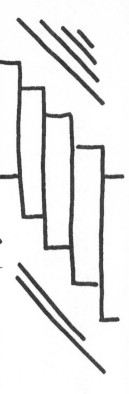

#61

How many miles long is the Great Wall of China?

Clue: If you walked at a speed of 5 miles per hour, it would take you 900 hours to walk the length of the Great Wall of China.

#63

The world's highest waterfall is Angel Falls in Venezuela. How high is Angel Falls?

Clue: A rock fell from the top of the waterfall at a speed of 50 feet per second. It took the rock 64 seconds to reach the bottom.

225 Fantastic Facts Math Word Problems

#66

How many dimples are on a golf ball?

Clue: If you have 2 dimples, a golf ball has 168 times as many dimples as you do.

#68

What is the diameter of the sun?

Clue: The diameter of the Earth is 7,926 miles. The sun's diameter is 72,330 miles more than 100 times that of Earth.

#65

How many workers were needed to build the Panama Canal?

Clue: The Panama Canal is 50 miles long. It took 840 workers for every mile of the canal.

#67

How many gallons was the largest milk shake?

Clue: A total of 2,000 people gathered and each drank 2 gallons of the shake. When they finished drinking, there were still 333 gallons of the shake left.

#70

The crocodile is the heaviest reptile. How much can a crocodile weigh?

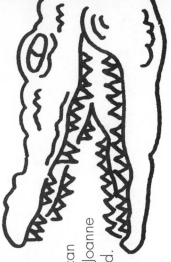

Clue: Joanne weighs 60 pounds. She has twin brothers who each weigh 85 pounds. A crocodile can weigh 5 times more than Joanne and her brothers combined.

#72

In how many movies did John Wayne star?

Clue: John Wayne began acting at age 19 and made his last movie at age 70. While he was an actor, Wayne starred in an average of 3 movies per year.

#69

How long is the ravine in the Grand Canyon?

Clue: Sue rode her horse at a speed of 15 miles per hour. She began on one end of the Grand Canyon and rode for 14 hours. At that point, she was just 7 miles from the other side of the ravine.

#71

The python is the longest snake. How long can a python be?

Clue: If you lay 7 children who are all 5 feet tall head to toe, their total length is 3 feet longer than a full-grown python.

#74

How many dreams does the average person have in a leap year?

Clue: The average person has 4 dreams per night.

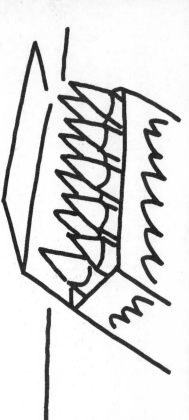

#76

How many crayons can the Crayola Company produce in two weeks?

Clue: Crayola can produce 5 million crayons every day.

#73

How many days did it take Christopher Columbus to cross the Atlantic Ocean?

Clue: It took Columbus 1,680 hours to cross the Atlantic Ocean.

#75

What is the greatest number of tattoos anyone has ever had?

Clue: If you were tattooed 1,000 times per day, it would take 2 weeks to equal the number of tattoos this person had.

#78

The national park that gets the most visitors every year is the Great Smoky Mountains National Park in Tennessee. How many people visit the park each year?

Clue: During an average month, about 770,000 people visit the park.

#80

How many plays did Lope de Vega write?

Clue: If you wrote 3 plays every month, it would take you 50 years to write the same number that de Vega wrote.

#77

How many earthquakes occur in the world every year?

Clue: About 960 earthquakes take place per week.

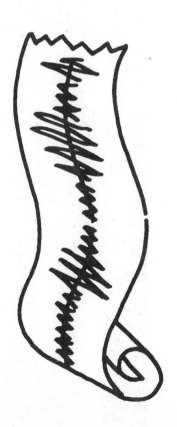

#79

What is the record for the most raw eggs eaten in one second?

Clue: If a hen lays 1 egg every 5 minutes, it would take the hen 1 hour, 5 minutes to lay this many eggs.

#82

How deep is the Pacific Ocean?

Clue: If a submarine dives 25 feet every second, it will take 8 minutes, 37 seconds to reach the ocean floor.

#84

To the closest dollar amount, how much does it cost a family to care for a dog?

Clue: Sal makes $25,600 per year. If he wants to care for a dog, it will cost him 3 months' salary.

#81

Mount Waialeale in Hawaii gets a lot of rainfall. How many inches does it get per year?

Clue: Mount Waialeale gets 38 inches of rain per month.

#83

What was the diameter of the biggest bubble-gum bubble?

Clue: The radius of the biggest bubble-gum bubble was equal to (3.5 x 3) inches. The radius of a circle is half the length of the diameter.

#86

How many peanuts does it take to make a 12-ounce jar of peanut butter?

Clue: It takes 274 peanuts to make a 6-ounce jar of peanut butter.

#85

How often does the average American move in a lifetime?

Clue: Alex lived to be 88 years old and moved once every 4 years. In total, she moved twice as many times as the average American.

#88

How fast can long-legged spiders crawl?

Clue: Dante rides his bike 8 miles per hour, racing the fastest spider. After a half-hour, the spider is 1 mile ahead of him.

#87

How many miles per hour can a peregrine falcon dive?

Clue: A peregrine falcon can dive 1 mile in about 20 seconds.

#90

How many inches long were the largest dinosaur footprints ever found?

Clue: Anna is 4 feet, 1 inch tall. She could lie in one of these footprints with 4 inches to spare.

#92

The record for the deepest dive without equipment was set by Francisco Ferreras of Cuba. How many feet down did he dive?

Clue: If Ferreras had gone 1 foot deeper, he would have reached 143 yards.

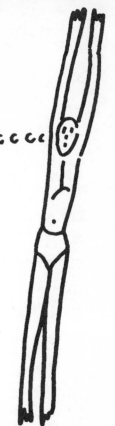

#89

St. Petersburg, Florida, set the record for the most sunny days in a row. How many days in a row were sunny?

Clue: It was sunny in St. Petersburg for 109 weeks and 5 days in a row.

#91

The tallest tree was a eucalyptus in Australia. How tall was it?

Clue: A football field is 100 yards long. The height of the eucalyptus tree was 153 feet more than the length of a football field.

How long was the longest swimming pool?

Clue: Marty swam the length of the pool 6 times, which was equal to 10,530 feet.

How many bones are babies born with?

Clue: There are 13 babies in a room at Strong Hospital. There are a total of 4,550 bones in the room.

What is the greatest number of piercings anyone has ever had?

Clue: If 1 piercing cost $20, it would cost $2,740 to have this many piercings.

Ronald King set a record for playing and winning the most checker games at once. How many did he win?

Clue: There are 24 checkers needed for a game. To set the record, King needed to use 9,240 checkers.

#98

How many pitches does the average baseball last in a major league game?

Clue: In a game in which 300 pitches are thrown, 50 baseballs should be used.

#100

How much did the largest brussels sprout weigh?

Clue: If you ate a pound of the largest brussels sprout every 2 days, it would take you 322 days to eat all of it.

#97

How many McDonald's restaurants are there in the United States?

Clue: If you purchased a 6-piece chicken McNugget from every McDonald's in the United States, you would have 84,000 pieces.

#99

Wyoming is the state in which the fewest people live. How many people live in Wyoming?

Clue: Thirty-two million people live in California, which has 64 times more people than Wyoming.

#101

The slowest mammal is the three-toed sloth from tropical South America. How far can it move in one hour?

Clue: In 2 full days, the sloth can travel 336 feet.

#102

How many words can one pencil write?

Clue: You could write the sentence "I never lose my pencil" 9,000 times with the same pencil.

#103

How many weeks does it take a human to shed one layer of skin?

Clue: A human sheds 13 layers of skin every year.

#104

How many times can a humming-bird flap its wings in one second?

Clue: In 30 seconds, a hummingbird can flap its wings 2,250 times.

#106

How many cars can fit in the parking lot of Minnesota's Mall of America?

Clue: If 24,000 people go to the mall with 3 people traveling in every car, 4,750 parking spots would be left unused.

#108

How fast can a turkey run?

Clue: Los Angeles is about 340 miles from San Francisco. If a turkey ran at its top speed the entire time and took a 2-hour rest stop, it would take 19 hours for it to run from San Francisco to Los Angeles.

#105

The windiest city in the United States is Great Falls, Montana. What is the average wind speed in Great Falls?

Clue: Richard is driving his car 52 miles per hour, which is 4 times greater than the average wind speed in Great Falls.

#107

How many movies does the average person see in a theater each year?

Clue: Last year Marcus saw 1 movie every month. Melissa went to see just 2 movies the entire year. Together, they saw twice the average number of movies 1 person sees.

#110

Shannon Lucid spent more days in outer space than any other astronaut. How many days did she spend in space?

Clue: Lucid spent a total of 5,352 hours in space.

#112

What is the record for the greatest number of haircuts given by one barber in an hour?

Clue: Trevor Mitchell set the record. In 1 hour he gave a haircut every 3 minutes, 20 seconds.

#109

How long was the longest bicycle wheelie in hours and minutes?

Clue: The longest bicycle wheelie was 640 minutes.

#111

Michael Kearney was the youngest person to graduate from college. How old was he when he graduated?

Clue: Usually college graduates are about 21 years old. Two months after Kearney graduated, he was half that age.

#114

What was the longest recorded distance a cherry pit was spit?

Clue: If the pit had traveled another foot, it would have gone 32 yards.

#116

Kevin Olmstead won the largest prize in game show history. How much money did he win, in dollars?

Clue: If he were paid in quarters, he would have received 8,720,000.

#113

How many pounds did the heaviest frog weigh?

Clue: The heaviest frog weighed 128 ounces.

#115

The tallest mountain in the United States is California's Mt. Whitney. In yards, how tall is it?

Clue: Mt. Whitney is 14,946 feet high.

#118

Women live the longest in Japan. On average, how long do women in Japan live?

Clue: Three Japanese women lived to be 86, 81, and 79 years old. The average life span of those 3 is the same as for all the women of Japan.

#120

How much water do you use every time you take a 10-minute shower?

Clue: You use about 1 gallon of water for every 15 seconds you spend in the shower.

#117

How much did a movie ticket cost in 1940?

Clue: Francisco has 1 quarter, 2 nickels, 1 dime, and 5 pennies. In the year 1940, that would have been enough money to pay for 2 movie tickets.

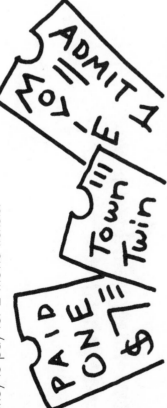

#119

How fast can a dragonfly fly?

Clue: A dragonfly can fly 12 miles in 20 minutes.

#122

How long was the longest beard?

Clue: An average beard is about 2.1 inches long. The longest beard was 100 times longer than that.

#124

How many feet of earthworms do baby robins eat every day?

Clue: If a robin eats earthworms that are 2 inches long, it will eat 84 in a day.

#121

How many times does the average person blink in one hour?

Clue: The average person blinks once every 5 seconds.

#123

How many feet long is your small intestine?

Clue: Your large intestine is 60 inches long. Your small intestine is 5 times longer than your large intestine.

#125

How tall was the tallest scarecrow, in feet and inches?

Clue: The tallest scarecrow was 18 times taller than a 69-inch scarecrow.

#126

William Henry Harrison served the shortest term as U.S. president. How many days did Harrison serve?

Clue: Harrison served for 4 weeks, 72 hours.

#127

How far can a kangaroo jump, in feet?

Clue: A kangaroo can jump 8 yards, 72 inches.

#128

The world's heaviest snowfall fell on Silver Lake, Colorado, in 1921. How many feet of snow fell?

Clue: Over a period of 24 hours, it snowed at a rate of 1 inch every 20 minutes.

#130

How many letters are used in the Hawaiian alphabet?

Clue: The Hawaiian alphabet only uses 6/13 the number of letters used in the 26-letter alphabet.

#132

Tatum O'Neal is the youngest actor to win an Academy Award. How old was she when she won?

Clue: Jessica Tandy was 80 years old when she won her Academy Award. When O'Neal won, she was 1/8 as old as Tandy was when she won hers.

#129

How many quills does the average porcupine have?

Clue: Porter the Porcupine is low on quills. He has 10,000 quills, which is only 1/3 as many as the average porcupine.

#131

How long does the average dog live?

Clue: The average dog lives 4/5 as long as the average cat. The average cat lives 15 years.

#134

What is the record time for eating 30 hot dogs?

Clue: The record holder ate 1 hot dog every 2 2/15 seconds, for a total of 30 dogs.

#136

How many pairs of legs can a centipede have?

Clue: A group of 10 people only have 1/7 the number of legs that a centipede can have.

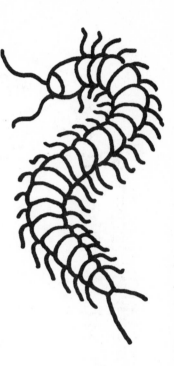

#133

How many people in the United States speak Spanish?

Clue: About 40 million people speak Spanish in Spain. The United States has 9/20 as many Spanish speakers as Spain does.

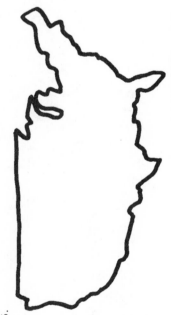

#135

The tallest structure in the United States is the TV Tower in Blanchard, North Dakota. How tall is it?

Clue: Freddy threw a ball that went 1/8 as high as the tower. The ball went 258 feet into the air.

#138

How much does the Statue of Liberty weigh?

Clue: Harry guessed that the Statue of Liberty weighed 536 tons. His guess was 8/3 more than the statue's actual weight.

#140

How many eyes can a scorpion have?

Clue: You have 1/6 as many eyes as a scorpion can have.

#137

Rotterdam has the busiest shipping port in the world. How many ships come in and out each year?

Clue: In a day, 100 ships docked, which is 1/300 the number of ships that use the port over the course of a year.

#139

How many languages are spoken throughout the world?

Clue: Shannon speaks 25 languages. She speaks 1/120 of the world's languages.

#142

How many diapers does the average baby use?

Clue: Dan was a quick learner. He used 1,125 diapers, which is just 1/4 that of the average baby.

#144

How fast can a cheetah run?

Clue: Carl can run 12 miles per hour. He can run only 1/5 as fast as a cheetah can run.

#141

In New York City, how many people live on each square mile of land?

Clue: A total of 6,000 people live on every 1/4 square mile.

#143

How many rivers does the Amazon River cross?

Clue: Tabitha traveled down the Amazon and counted 220 rivers along the way, but her guide told her she only saw 1/5 of the rivers that the Amazon crosses.

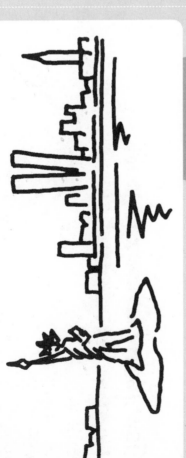

How long was the longest recorded case of the hiccups?

Clue: If you hiccuped for 2 years straight, that would be just 1/34 as long as the longest case of hiccups.

How long was the longest unicycle ride?

Clue: When the unicyclist had ridden 2,174 miles, he had traveled 2/3 of the way.

The deepest lake in the United States is Crater Lake in Oregon. How deep is Crater Lake?

Clue: When a fish is swimming at the midpoint between the lake's floor and the surface, the fish is 966 feet deep.

How many crime novels did Agatha Christie write?

Clue: Jane read 13 of Christie's crime novels, which is only 1/6 of the total that Christie wrote.

#150

How fast does ketchup travel as it's leaving the bottle?

Clue: If a snail can travel 15 miles per year, ketchup travels $5/3$ as fast.

#152

How far was the longest Frisbee throw?

Clue: When the longest Frisbee throw was $3/4$ of the way there, it had traveled 492 feet.

#149

How many stars are there in the galaxy?

Clue: On a given night, if you can see 100,000 stars, you can only see $1/2{,}000{,}000$ of all the stars.

#151

Compared to others around the world, Norwegians spend the most money on books per year. How much do Norwegians spend on books?

Clue: Americans spend an average of $90 per year on books. That is $9/13$ of the amount of money that Norwegians spend on books.

#154

How many hairs does the average adult head have?

Clue: Frank's father started balding and has only 7/8 as much hair as the average person. He now has 87,500 hairs on his head.

#156

The largest U.S. war ship afloat today is the U.S.S. ENTERPRISE. How long is it?

Clue: Colby walked 5/7 of the way across the ship and then stopped. He then started walking again and went another 8/77 of the way across. At that point he had walked 900 feet.

#153

How many calories can you burn while horseback riding for an hour?

Clue: You can burn 210 calories biking for an hour. You can burn 3/5 as many calories biking as you can burn horseback riding.

#155

What was the length of the longest triple jump by a frog?

Clue: The record for a human triple jump is 60 feet, by Jonathan Edwards. A frog once jumped 3 feet more than 1/2 that distance.

#157

How many pounds of food can a wild elephant eat in a day?

Clue: If an elephant ate 150 pounds for breakfast and 200 pounds for lunch, it would have at that point eaten 7/10 of what it can eat in a day.

#158

How many sodas does the average person drink in a year?

Clue: Last year Gabby drank 125 root beers, 100 cokes, and no other soda. She drank only 3/8 the amount of soda that the average person drinks.

#159

How many inches long can a giraffe's tongue be?

Clue: One foot is 4/7 as long as a giraffe's tongue.

#160

How many words does the average high school graduate know?

Clue: Ben knows 11,700 words. Seneca knows 13,300 words. Together, they know ½ as many words as the average high school graduate does.

#162

How many islands are there in Hawaii?

Clue: Alexi has been to 51 Hawaiian islands. After she visits 10 more, she will have visited exactly ½ the islands.

#164

How many World Series have the Yankees won?

Clue: The Cardinals have won 9 World Series and the Mets have won 3. Together they have won $\frac{6}{13}$ the number that the Yankees have won.

#161

How high is Mount Everest?

Clue: Carlos climbed ½ way to the top of Mount Everest and then took a break. He continued climbing and climbed another ¼ of the way. When he finally stopped, he was 21,771 feet from the ground.

#163

The largest bird is the ostrich. How much can an ostrich weigh?

Clue: Binny weighs 102 pounds, and Elena weighs 68 pounds. Together they only weigh ½ of what an ostrich can weigh.

#165

Saturn is the planet with the most moons. How many moons does Saturn have?

Clue: Ashley spotted 6 of Saturn's moons with her high-powered telescope, but she did not see 2/3 of Saturn's moons.

#166

How old was the oldest woman ever to have a baby?

Clue: When the woman's daughter turned 9, she was 1/8 the age of her mother.

#167

How many days did it take to build the Empire State Building?

Clue: Anton began making his go-cart at noon on September 2 and finished at noon on November 23. The time it took him to build his go-cart is 1/5 of the time it took to build the entire Empire State Building.

#168

How long is the Statue of Liberty's nose?

Clue: The width of the Statue of Liberty's mouth is 3 feet. That is 2/3 the size of the length of her nose.

#170

How tall was the tallest sunflower?

Clue: The tallest giraffe was 6.09 meters, which is 1.08 meters shorter than the tallest sunflower.

#172

The widest tree in the world is a giant sequoia in California. How great is its diameter?

Clue: The diameter of the tree in Sandy's back yard is 7.63 feet. The largest sequoia has a diameter 29.67 feet greater than Sandy's tree.

#169

Key West, Florida, has the hottest average temperature in the United States. What is the average temperature in Key West?

Clue: The coldest city in the United States is Barrow, Alaska, which has an average temperature of 9.6 degrees. In Key West, the average temperature is 68.1 degrees warmer than it is in Barrow.

#171

The highest measure on the Richter scale resulted from a 1960 earthquake in Chile. How high did it measure?

Clue: A 1906 quake in San Francisco peaked at 8.3 but the Chilean earthquake was 1.2 higher on the scale.

225 Fantastic Facts Math Word Problems

#174

How many potatoes are grown in Idaho every year?

Clue: Enough potatoes are grown in Idaho for every state to have 0.54 billion potatoes.

#176

The longest suspension bridge in the North America is the Verrazano-Narrows bridge in New York City. How long is it?

Clue: A mile is 5,280 feet. The Verrazano-Narrows bridge is 0.8 miles long.

#173

How many feet of tape does a 60-minute audiocassette contain?

Clue: For every minute of the 60-minute cassette, there is 9.5 feet of tape.

#175

Mercury is the fastest moving planet. How many miles does Mercury travel per hour?

Clue: Pluto is the slowest moving planet. It travels about 10,000 miles per hour. Mercury travels 10.7 times faster than Pluto does.

#178

How many people speak Mandarin, the official spoken language of China?

Clue: Three hundred forty million people speak English as their first language. There are 2.56 times as many Mandarin speakers.

#180

How many times its own body weight can an ant lift?

Clue: An ant that weighs .015 ounces can lift something that weighs 0.75 ounces.

#177

How long is a marathon?

Clue: Ingrid ran a half-marathon. She ran 13.1 miles.

#179

Ty Cobb scored the most runs in baseball history. How many runs did he score?

Clue: Cobb played 3,034 games. He averaged 0.74 runs for every game in which he played.

(**Hint:** Round your answer to the nearest whole number.

#182

How many pounds of peanut butter does the average person eat in a year?

Clue: Last year Stu ate 10.08 pounds of peanut butter, which is 3 times more peanut butter than the average person eats in a year.

#184

The tallest buildings in the world are the Petronas Towers in Malaysia. How tall are they?

Clue: A helicopter flying 1.5 times higher than the towers is 2,224.5 feet in the air.

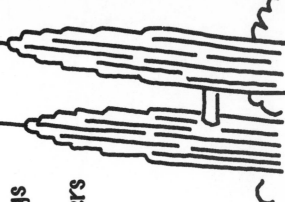

#181

What is the average number of people flying over the United States at any given time?

Clue: If there are 150,000 people flying, that is 2.5 times the average.

#183

How many gallons of water does the average American use daily?

Clue: Mike uses 109.8 gallons per day, which is only 0.6 times what the average American does.

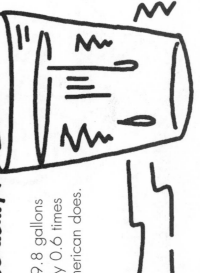

#186

How far can light travel in one second?

Clue: During a vacation, Cal traveled 1,862.12 miles to his destination and then the exact same distance back. In just one second, light can travel 50 times farther than the total distance Cal covered on his trip.

#188

How many times did tennis great Martina Navratilova win Wimbledon?

Clue: Steffi Graf won Wimbledon 7 times and Chris Everett won it 3 times. Navratilova won 0.9 times as much as Graf and Everett combined.

#185

How many cats are there in the United States?

Clue: There are 8 million more cats than dogs in the United States. There are 1.16 million dogs per state.

#187

How high can a puma jump?

Clue: Sally, Shirley, Suzie, and Sunny are quadruplets who are each 4.5 feet tall. A puma can jump 2 feet higher than their combined heights.

What was the minimum wage in 1938?

Clue: In 1938, employees who earned the minimum wage had to work 20 hours to earn $5.00.

How much did a gallon of gas cost in 1960?

Clue: Julio just bought 10 gallons of gas for $17.50. The price per gallon that Julio paid was $1.44 more than a gallon of gas cost in 1960.

The longest cave in the United States is Kentucky's Mammoth Cave. How long is it?

Clue: Amanda traveled 16.3 miles into the cave each day for 4 days in a row. At that point she still had 282.8 more miles to reach the end.

Approximately how many copies of his album, THRILLER, has Michael Jackson sold?

Clue: If Jackson has made just one penny for each album he has sold, he would have made $400,000.

225 Fantastic Facts Math Word Problems

#194

What is the speed of an average tornado?

Clue: Sammy is driving her car at a speed of 30 miles per hour. Sammy's speed is 75% of the speed of an average tornado.

#196

How many turkeys do Americans eat on Thanksgiving?

Clue: Americans eat 300 million turkeys per year. Of those turkeys, 15% are eaten on Thanksgiving.

#193

What percentage of mothers work outside the home?

Clue: In 1955, only 27% of mothers worked outside the home. Today, that number is three times as many.

#195

New Jersey is the state that recycles the most items. What percentage of recyclable items does New Jersey recycle?

Clue: Out of 300 recyclable items, New Jersey recycles 168 of them.

#197

How long is a squirrel expected to live?

Clue: A squirrel is expected to live 50% as long as a horse, which is expected to live for 20 years.

#198

How old was Bobby Fischer when he became the youngest chess champion ever?

Clue: Lou's grandmother is 70 years old. Bobby was only 20% as old as her when he became chess champ.

#199

What percentage of people ages 18 to 29 vote?

Clue: Out of 400 people ages 18 to 29, only 132 vote.

#200

What percentage of American homes have at least three televisions?

Clue: Out of every 50 American homes, 17 have at least 3 televisions.

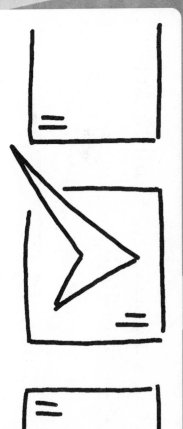

#202

What percentage of people say they are afraid of heights?

Clue: Out of 25 people, 8 say they are afraid of heights.

#204

How many people does the average McDonald's serve in one day?

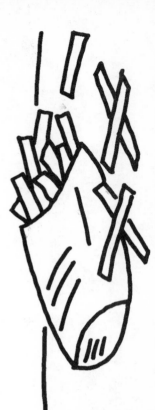

Clue: Eighty percent of the people who eat at McDonald's order french fries. The average McDonald's serves fries to 1,600 people every day.

#201

What percentage of people in the United States own computers?

Clue: Out of every 500 people in the United States, 145 own computers.

#203

What percentage of its life does an armadillo spend sleeping?

Clue: An armadillo will sleep for 24 out of 30 days.

#206

How many people read SEVENTEEN magazine each month?

Clue: *Boy's Life* has 1.2 million readers. *Boy's Life* has just 50% of the amount of readers that *Seventeen* does.

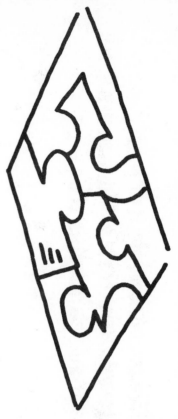

#208

How many pieces were there in the largest jigsaw puzzle?

Clue: When 50% of the jigsaw puzzle had been completed, 21,647 pieces had been used.

#205

How many different species of beetles are there?

Clue: Sammy the Scientist is trying to collect one of each different species of beetle. So far he has collected 14,500 different kinds, but he has completed only 5% of his job.

#207

How many malls are there in the United States?

Clue: Derek has been to 760 malls. He has been to 40% of the total malls in the country.

#210

Climax, Colorado, is the highest town in America. How many feet above sea level is it?

Clue: Angelina's town is 4,544 feet above sea level, which is 40% as high as Climax.

#212

What percentage of its money does the United States government spend on health care and social security?

Clue: For every dollar the government has, a quarter, a dime, a nickel, and a penny go to health care and social security.

#209

How many teeth do sharks go through in their life?

Clue: Sarah has a collection of 480 shark teeth. That is only 2% of how many one shark goes through in its life.

#211

What percentage of Earth's crust is made up of oxygen?

Clue: Earth's crust is made up of 28% silicon, 8% aluminum, and 17% other elements that are not oxygen.

How many home runs did baseball great Carl Yastrzemski hit?

Clue: Hank Aaron hit 755 home runs. If Yastrzemski had hit one more homer in his career, he would have hit 60% as many as Aaron.

How many different species can you see at the San Diego Zoo?

Clue: Jonathan went to the zoo and saw 50 species. A week later he went back and saw 150 more species. At that point Jonathan had seen 25% of all the species the zoo had on display.

The most hated chore for Americans is washing dishes. What percentage of people said washing dishes is their most hated chore?

Clue: While 8.5% of people said ironing was their most hated chore, twice as many people said they hated washing dishes.

How hot is the surface of the planet Venus?

Clue: One day it was 78 degrees in San Diego, 62 degrees in Wichita, and 40 degrees in Cleveland. When you add the temperature of these cities, the total is just 20% of the temperature on Venus.

#218

The world's largest island is Greenland. How many square miles is it?

Clue: If 168,000 square miles of Greenland are covered with snow, then 80% of the island is not covered in snow.

#220

The longest cycling race is the Tour de France. How long is it?

Clue: When Pierre had finished 1,491 miles of the race, his coach told him he had 40% of the race left.

#217

What percentage of people who live to be 100 years old are women?

Clue: Only 6 out of every 30 people who live to be 100 are males.

#219

What percentage of your body weight is made up of water?

Clue: If you weigh 110 pounds, 33 of those pounds do not come from water.

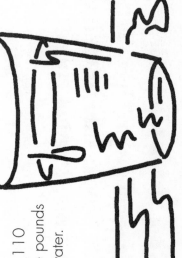

225 Fantastic Facts Math Word Problems

#222

How many days and hours did it take Apollo 11 to reach the moon?

Clue: The news showed 78 hours of the mission, which was 40% of the trip.

#224

How many tons did the largest meteorite ever to hit Earth weigh?

Clue: A meteorite that weighs 50% as much as the largest one weighs 65,000 pounds.

#221

The oldest living tree in the United States is a California bristlecone pine tree. How many years old is it?

Clue: Richard is 564 months old. He is 1% as old as the tree.

#223

How fast can a sailfish swim?

Clue: Michelle was driving her car 15.5 miles per hour, which is 25% as fast as a sailfish can swim.

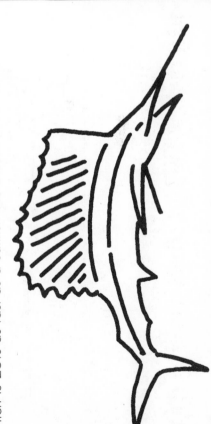

Using two of the operations listed, create your own word problem about a fantastic fact!

- addition
- division
- percentage
- money
- subtraction
- fractions
- time
- average
- multiplication
- decimals
- measurement

Using four of the operations listed, create your own word problem about a fantastic fact!

- addition
- division
- percentage
- money
- subtraction
- fractions
- time
- average
- multiplication
- decimals
- measurement

How long is the U.S.-Canadian border?

Clue: Donovan traveled 75% of the length of the U.S.-Canadian border. He paid a penny for every mile he went in tolls and ended up paying $29.91 for the trip.

Using three of the operations listed, create your own word problem about a fantastic fact!

- addition
- division
- percentage
- money
- subtraction
- fractions
- time
- average
- multiplication
- decimals
- measurement

Answers

1. 4,000 feet
2. 710 pounds
3. 2,260 pounds
4. 38,387 points
5. 4,145 miles
6. 566 people
7. 300 feet
8. 250,000 Native Americans
9. 6,208 square miles
10. 642 stitches
11. 138 million people
12. 151 skyscrapers
13. 43 muscles
14. 8,238 people
15. 1979
16. 3 hours, 48 minutes
17. 68 feet, 9 inches
18. 15 feet, 7 inches
19. 38 videos
20. $772 million
21. 1969
22. 1884
23. 70 years old
24. 29 stars
25. 8 presidents
26. 1,450 feet
27. 500,000 people
28. 27 million people
29. 367 feet
30. 924 pounds
31. 1850
32. 1290
33. 91 years
34. 122 years old
35. 42 years old
36. $16,029
37. 660 home runs
38. 1795
39. 45 miles per hour

40. 9 ounces
41. 50 years
42. 120 feet
43. 188 decibels
44. 478,800 times
45. $75 million
46. 6,500 feet
47. 333 squares
48. 100 people
49. 1,500 volcanoes
50. 35,000 radio stations
51. 4,400 pounds
52. 16,250 miles
53. 1,960 calories
54. 260,000 pounds
55. 11,000 pounds
56. 105 feet
57. 105 inches
58. 675,000 Wal-Mart workers
59. 840 people
60. 60,000 pounds
61. 4,500 miles
62. 1,600,000 miles
63. 3,200 feet
64. 1,860 stairs
65. 42,000 workers
66. 336 dimples
67. 4,333 gallons
68. 864,930 miles
69. 217 miles
70. 1,150 pounds
71. 32 feet
72. 153 movies
73. 70 days
74. 1,464 dreams
75. 14,000 tattoos
76. 70 million crayons
77. 49,920 earthquakes
78. 9,240,000 visitors

79. 13 eggs
80. 1,800 plays
81. 456 inches
82. 12,925 feet
83. 21 inches
84. $6,400
85. 11 times
86. 548 peanuts
87. 180 miles per hour
88. 10 miles per hour
89. 768 days
90. 53 inches
91. 453 feet
92. 428 feet
93. 137 piercings
94. 1,755 feet
95. 385 games
96. 350 bones
97. 14,000 McDonald's
98. 6 pitches
99. 500,000 people
100. 161 pounds
101. 7 feet
102. 45,000 words
103. 4 weeks
104. 75 times
105. 13 miles per hour
106. 12,750 cars
107. 7 movies
108. 20 miles per hour
109. 10 hours, 40 minutes
110. 223 days
111. 10 years, 4 months
112. 18 haircuts
113. 8 pounds
114. 95 feet
115. 4,982 yards
116. $2,180,000
117. $0.25

118. 82 years
119. 36 miles per hour
120. 40 gallons
121. 720 times
122. 17 feet, 6 inches
123. 25 feet
124. 14 feet
125. 103 feet, 6 inches
126. 31 days
127. 30 feet
128. 6 feet
129. 30,000 quills
130. 12 letters
131. 12 years
132. 10 years old
133. 18 million people
134. 64 seconds
135. 2,064 feet
136. 70 pairs
137. 30,000 ships
138. 201 tons
139. 3,000 languages
140. 12 eyes
141. 24,000 people
142. 4,500 diapers
143. 1,100 rivers
144. 60 miles per hour
145. 1,932 feet
146. 68 years
147. 78 crime novels
148. 3,261 miles
149. 200 billion stars
150. 25 miles per year
151. $130
152. 656 feet
153. 350 calories
154. 100,000 hairs
155. 33 feet
156. 1,100 feet

157. 500 pounds
158. 600 sodas
159. 21 inches
160. 50,000 words
161. 29,028 feet
162. 122 islands
163. 340 pounds
164. 26 World Series
165. 18 moons
166. 63 years old
167. 410 days
168. 4 feet, 6 inches
169. 77.7 degrees
170. 7.17 meters
171. 9.5
172. 37.3 feet
173. 570 feet
174. 27 billion potatoes
175. 107,000 miles per hour
176. 4,224 feet
177. 26.2 miles
178. 870.4 million
179. 2,245 runs
180. 50 times
181. 60,000 people
182. 3.36 pounds
183. 183 gallons
184. 1,483 feet
185. 66 million cats
186. 186,212 miles
187. 20 feet
188. 9 times
189. 348 miles
190. $0.25 per hour
191. 40 million copies
192. $0.31 per gallon
193. 81%
194. 40 miles per hour
195. 56%

196. 45 million turkeys
197. 10 years
198. 14 years old
199. 33%
200. 34%
201. 29%
202. 32%
203. 80%
204. 2,000 people
205. 290,000 species
206. 2.4 million readers
207. 1,900 malls
208. 43,294 pieces
209. 24,000 teeth
210. 11,360 feet
211. 47%
212. 41%
213. 17%
214. 452 home runs
215. 900 degrees
216. 800 species
217. 80%
218. 840,000 square miles
219. 70%
220. 2,485 miles
221. 4,700 years old
222. 8 days, 3 hours
223. 62 miles per hour
224. 65 tons
225. 3,988 miles